D IS IS DRA ING OOK
B LONG TO

____

____

____

We have created a schematic guide
How to draw step by step in a sketchbook
You draw dogs with six steps on the first page, and on
the second page, you draw and color the dog

By following the steps
With repetition and try and with time
You will find that you learn quickly

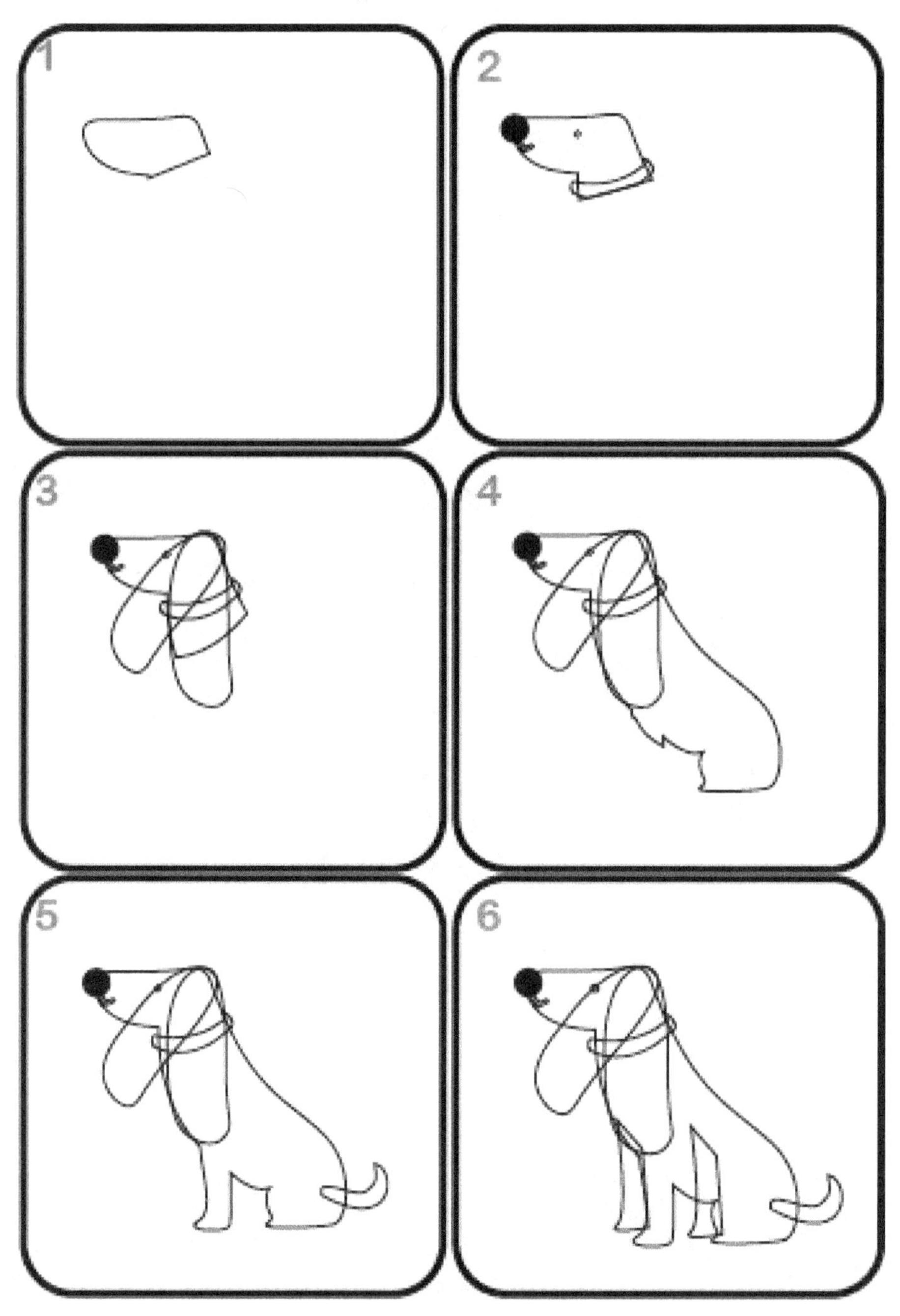

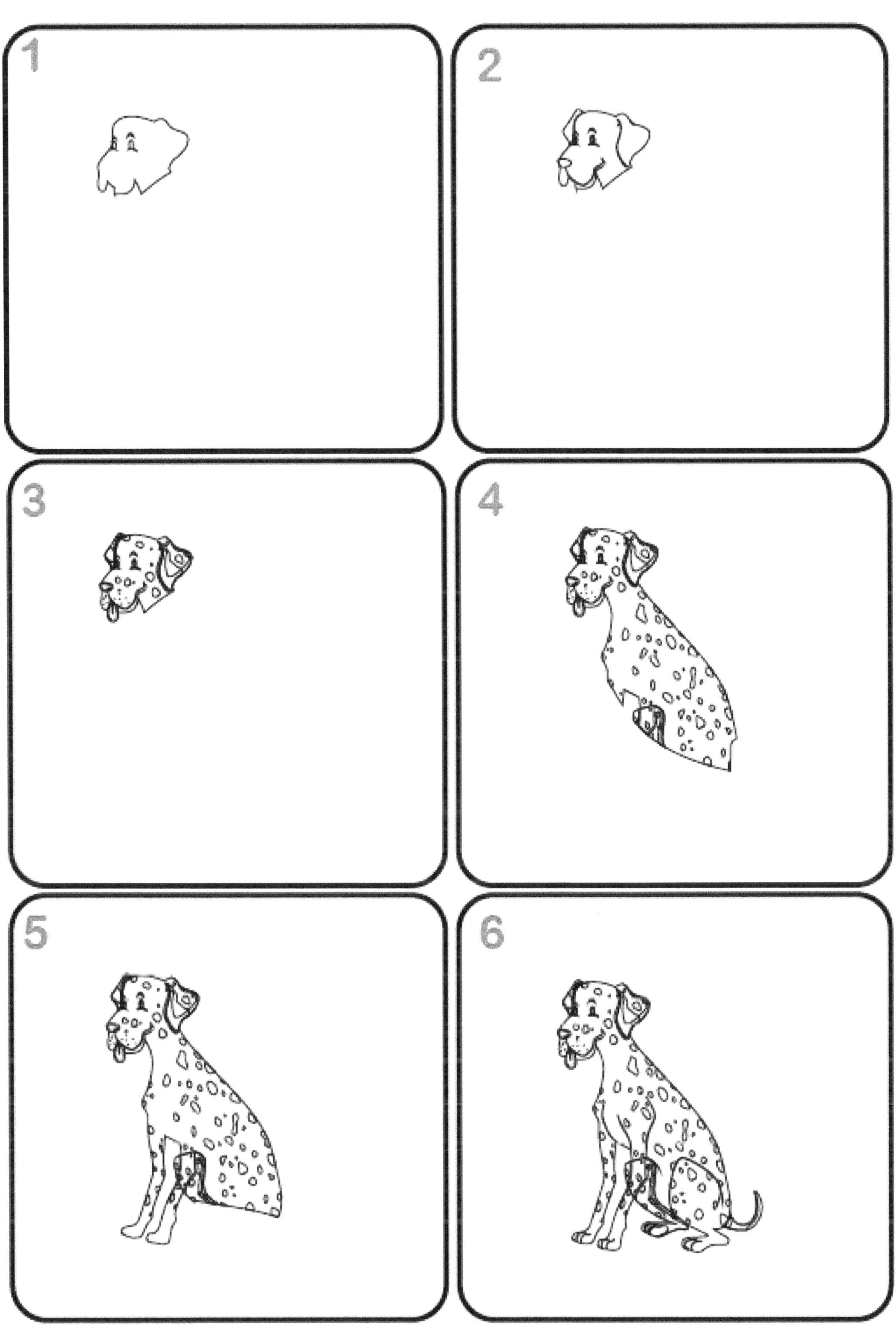

1
2
3
4
5
6

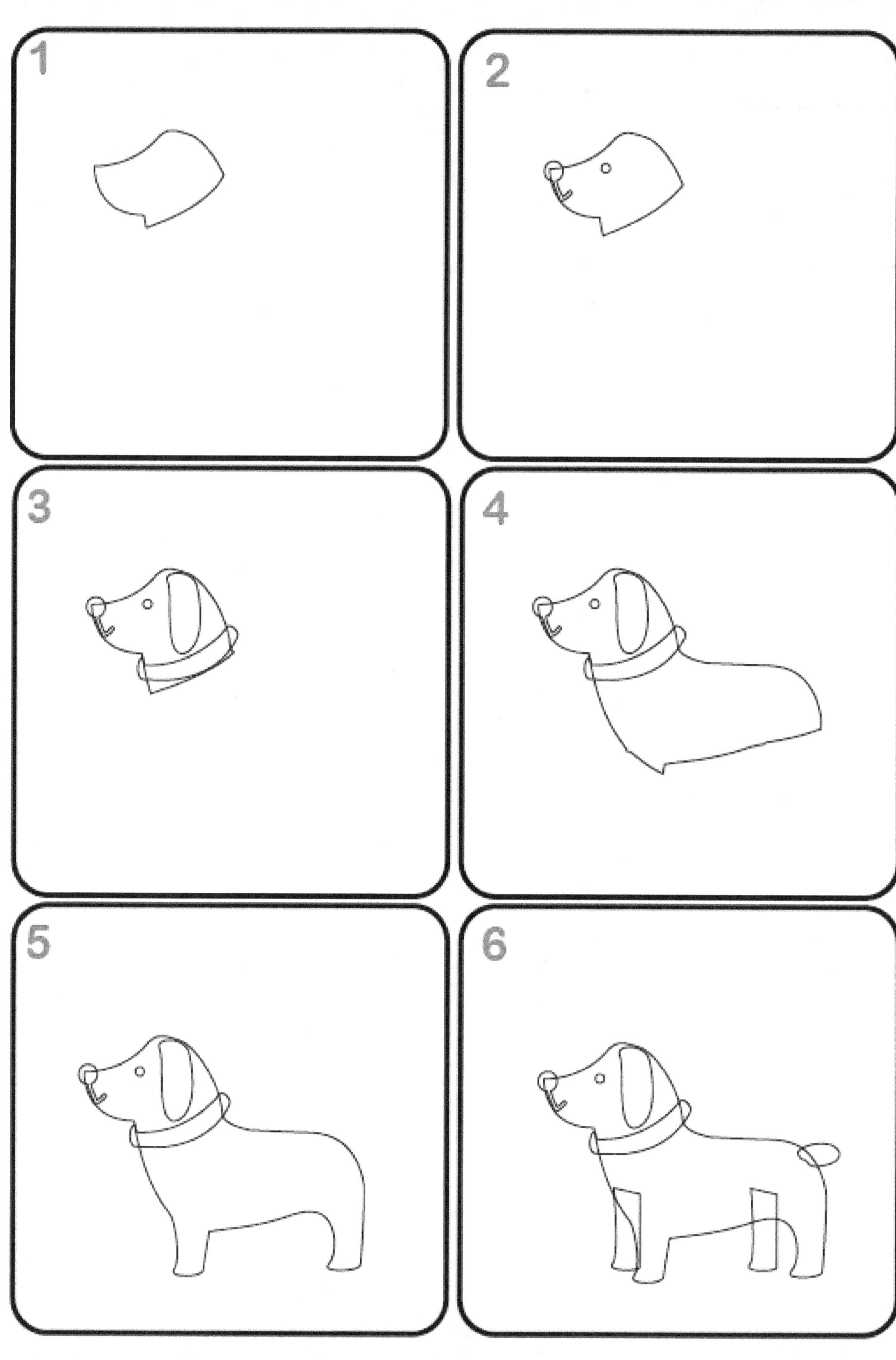

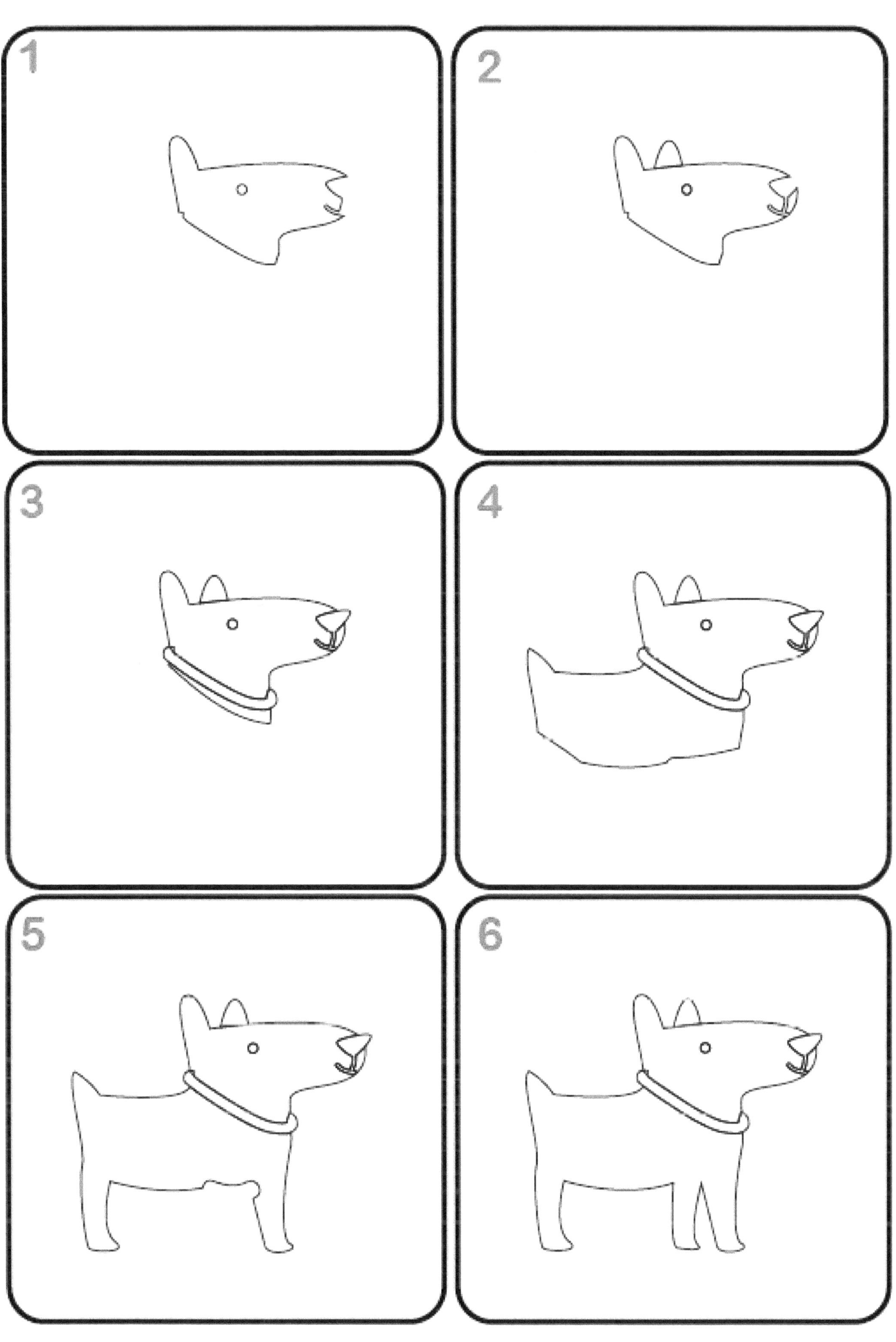

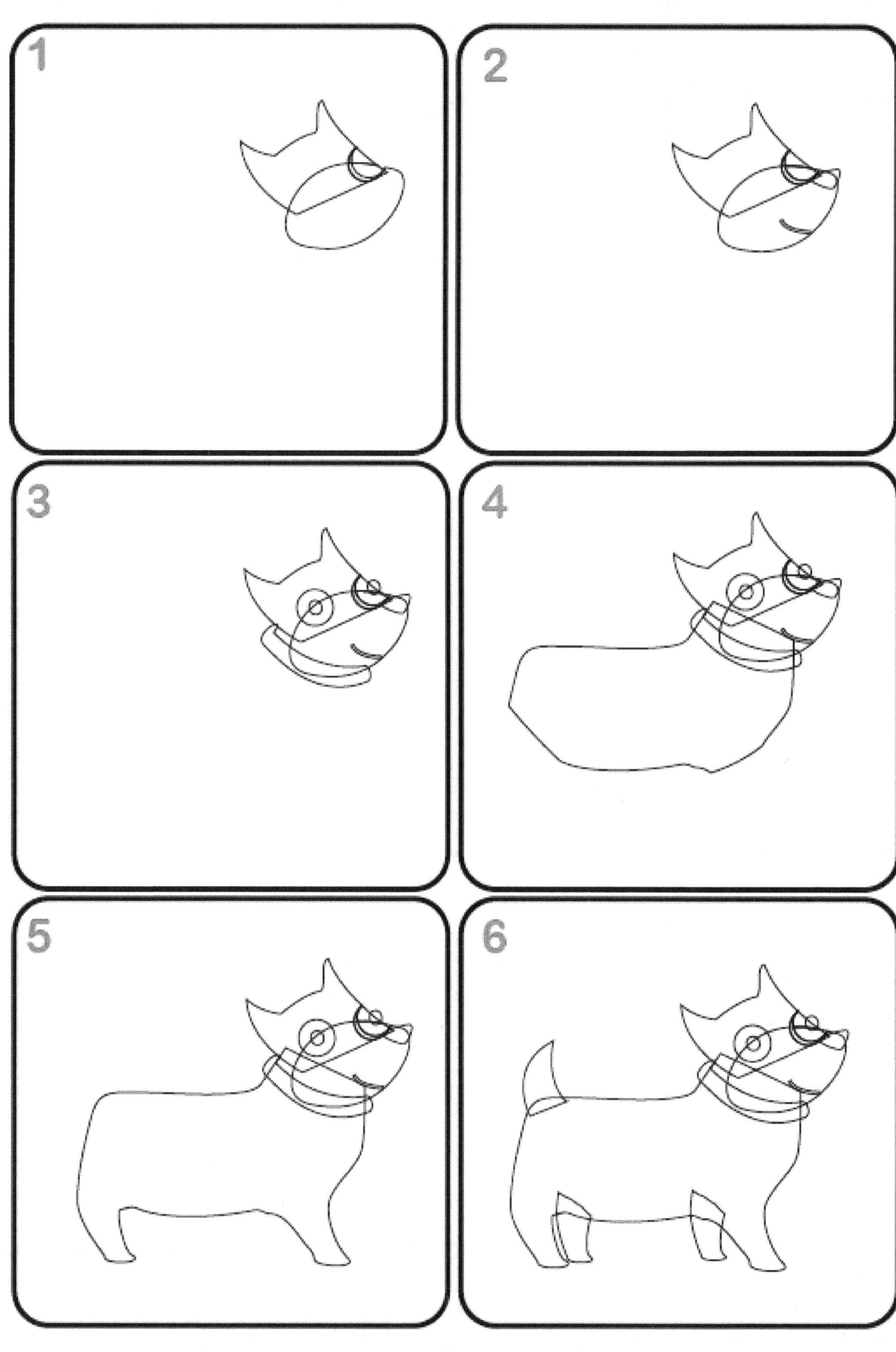

1
2
3
4
5
6

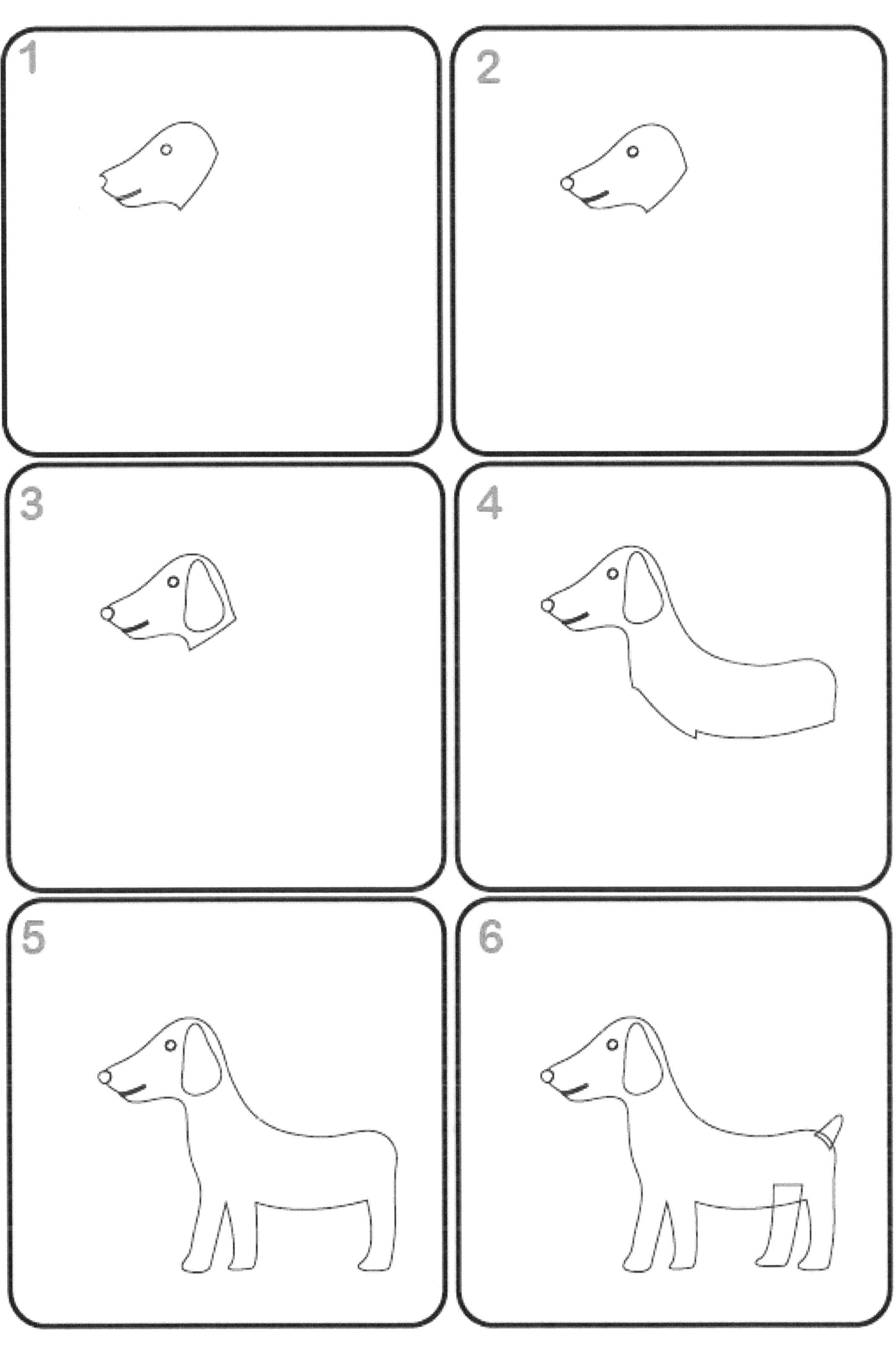

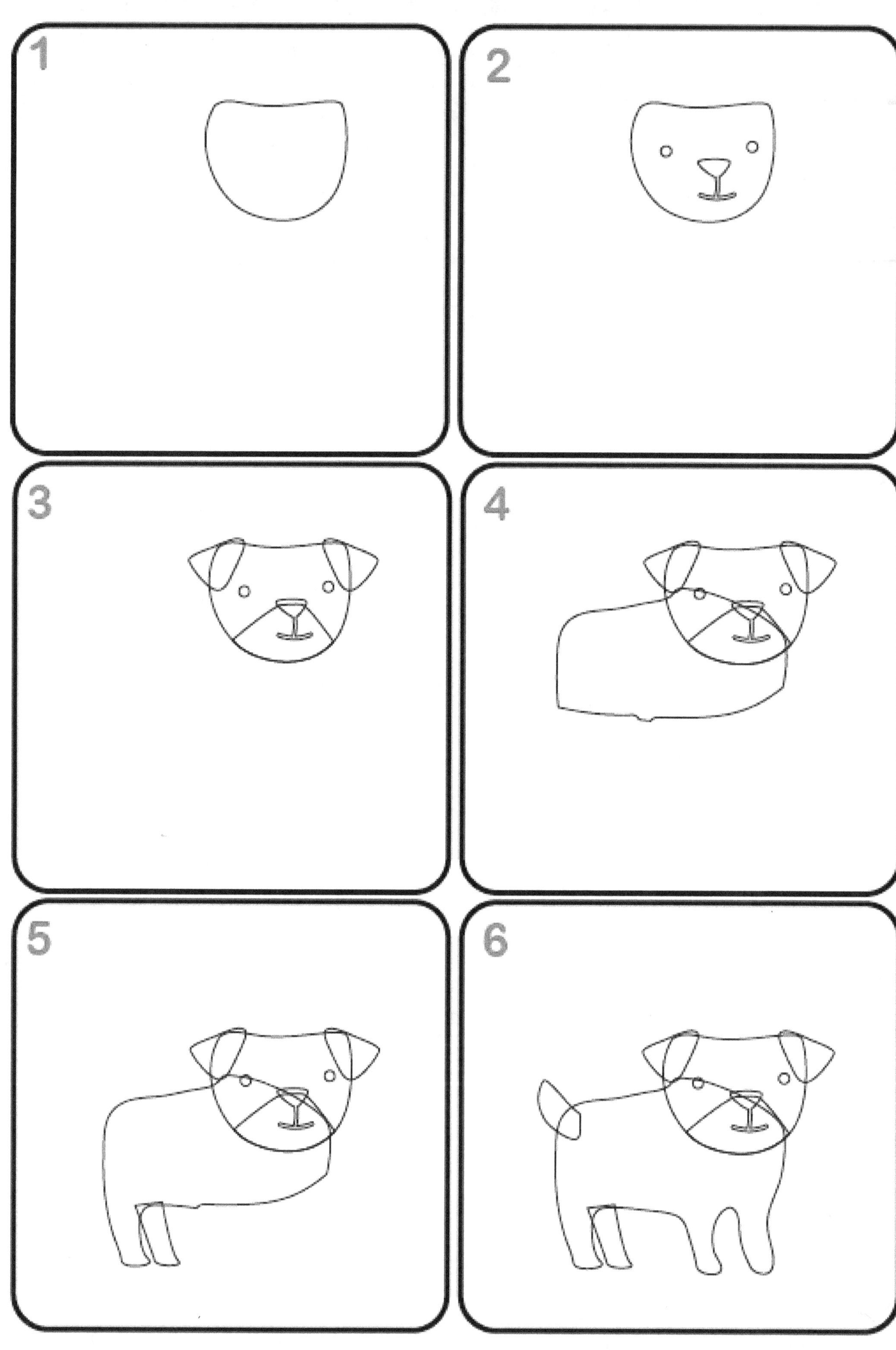

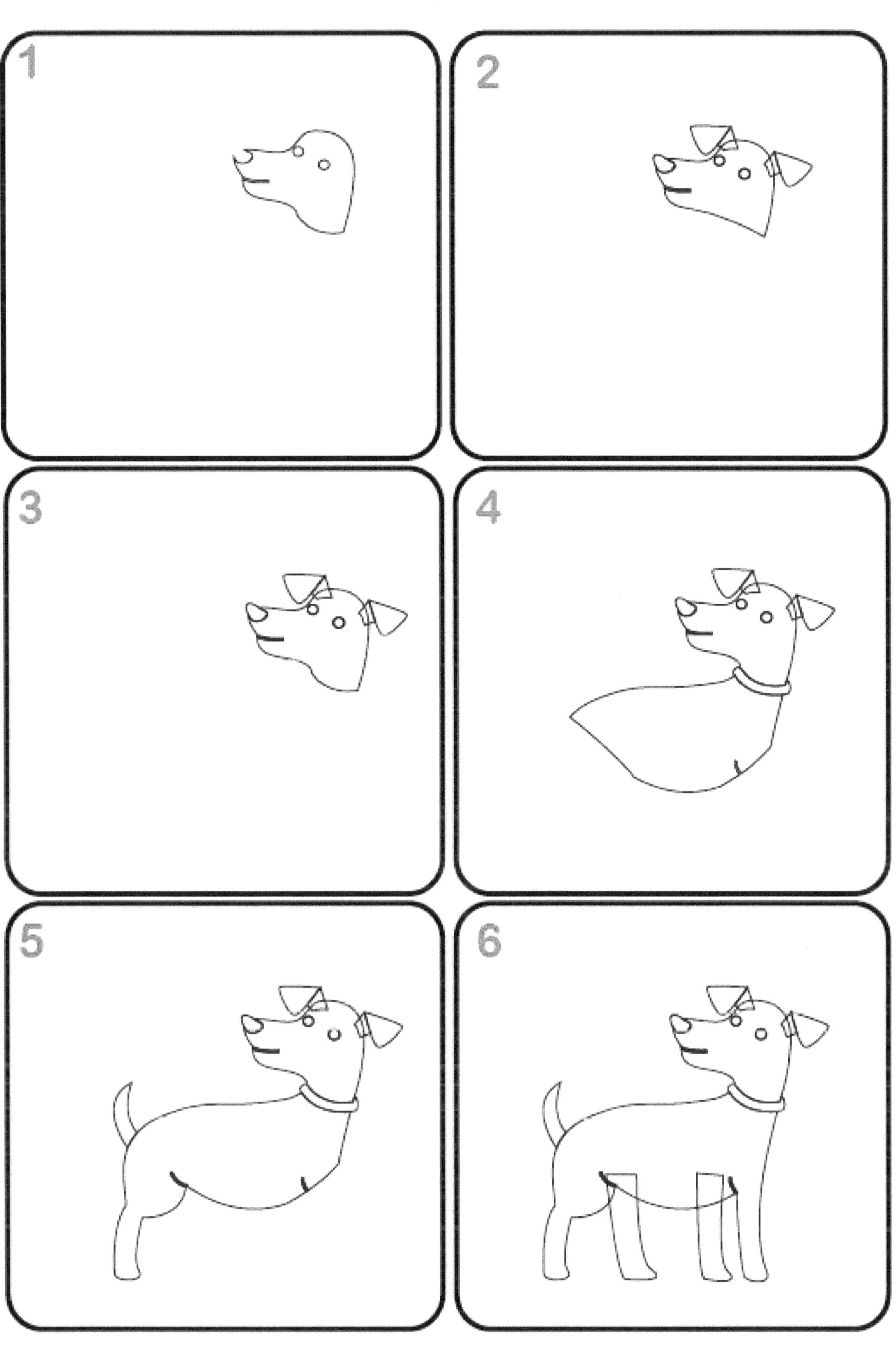

1
2
3
4
5
6

1
2
3
4
5
6

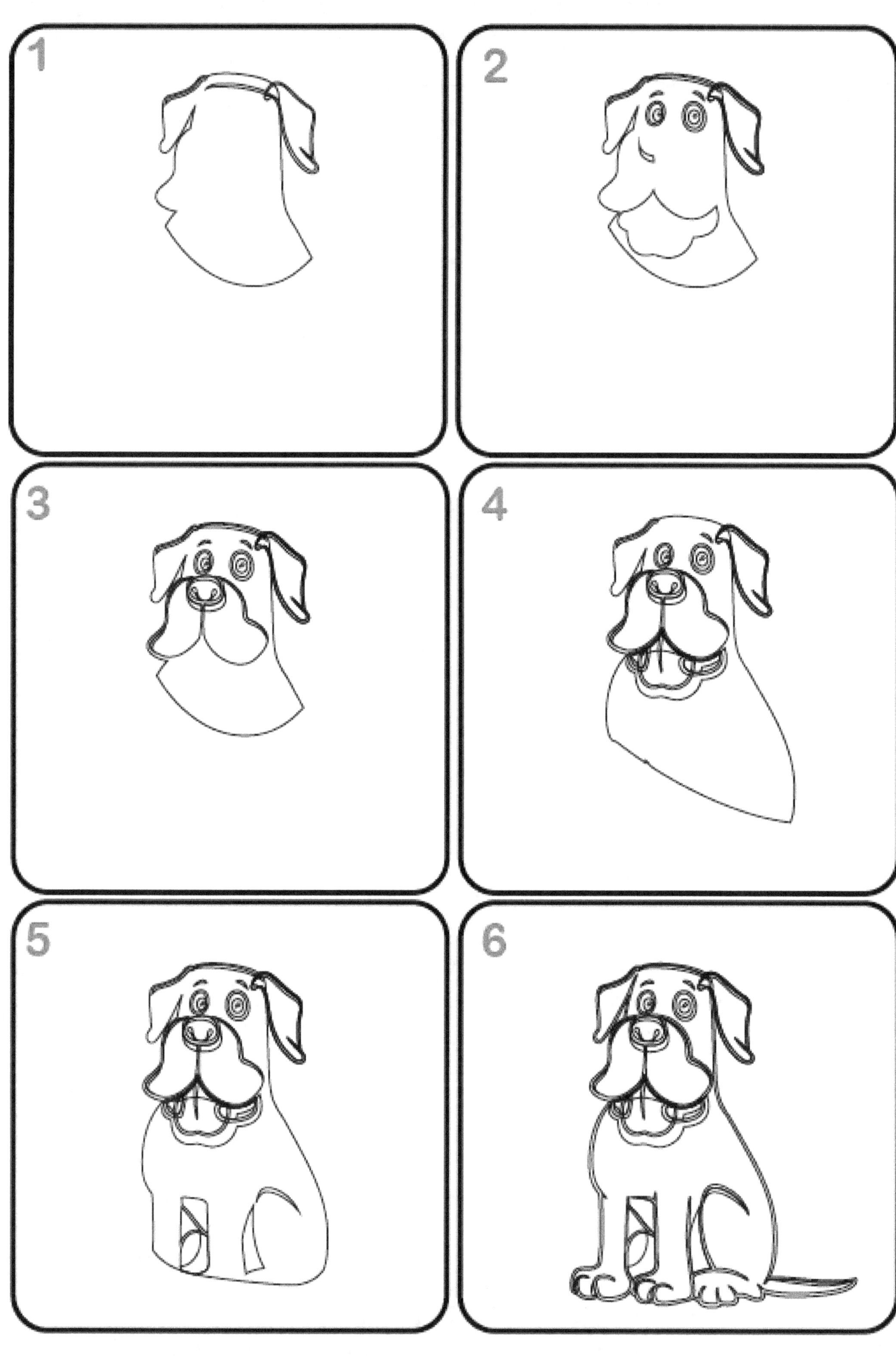

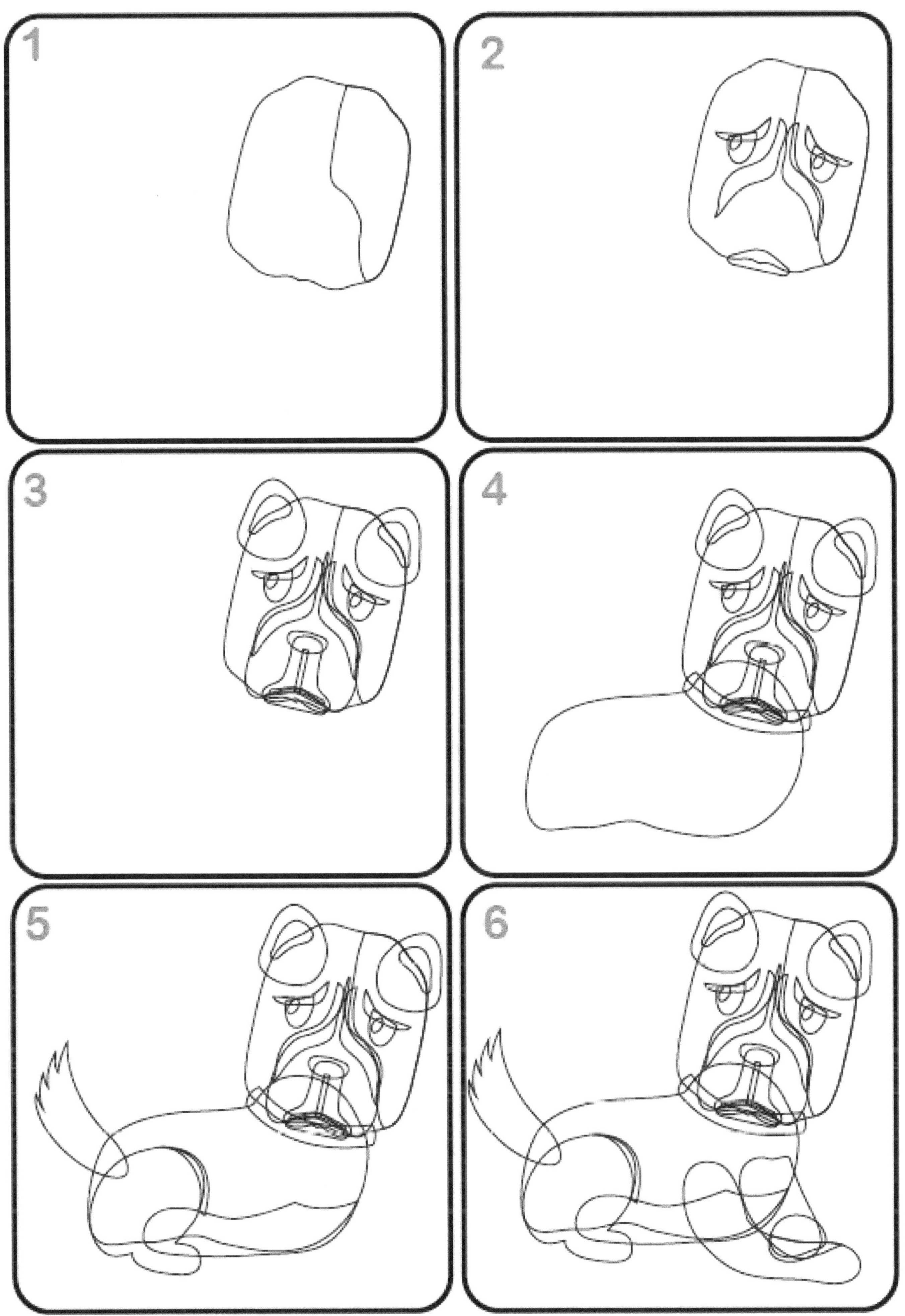

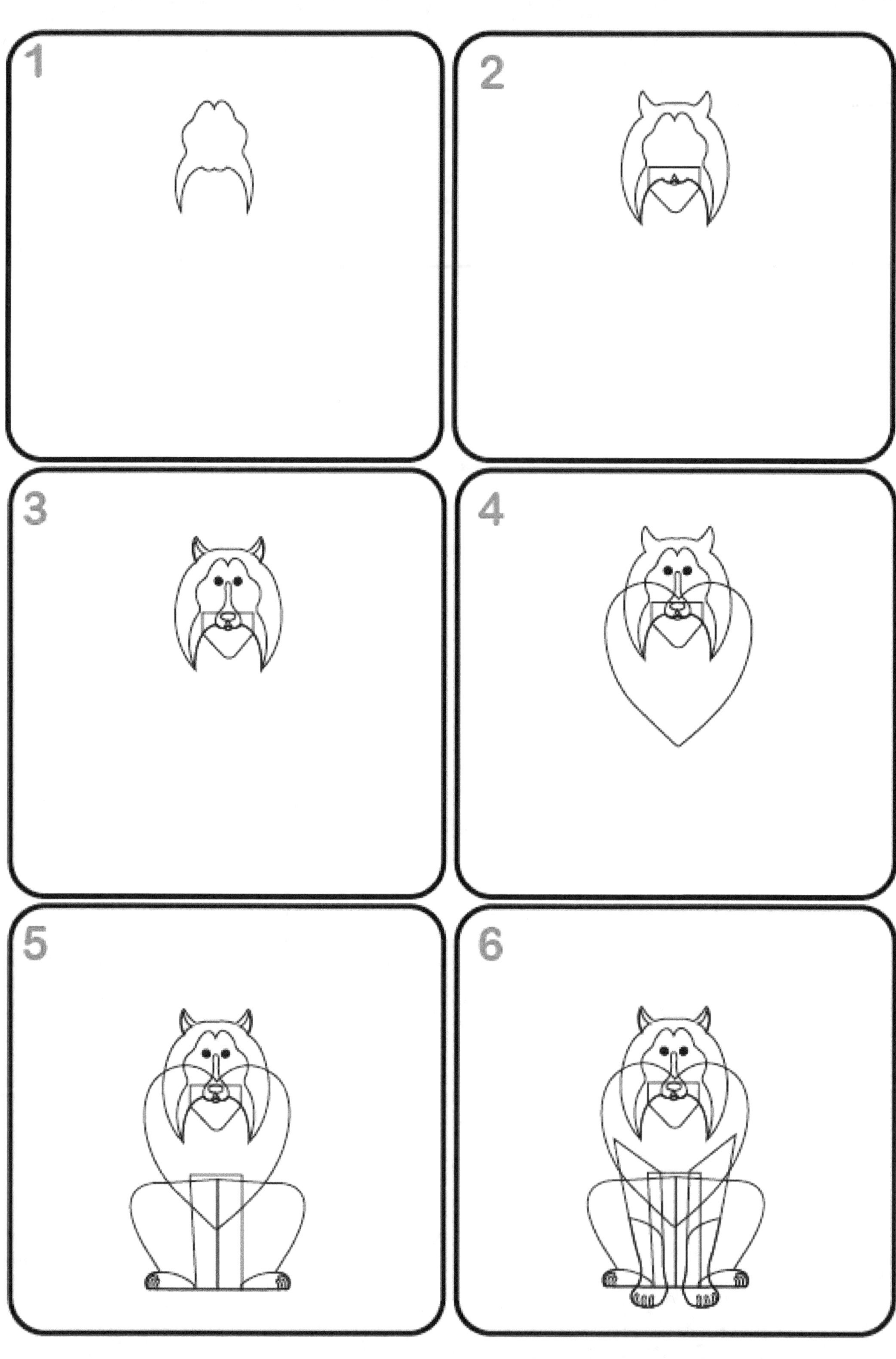

1
2
3
4
5
6

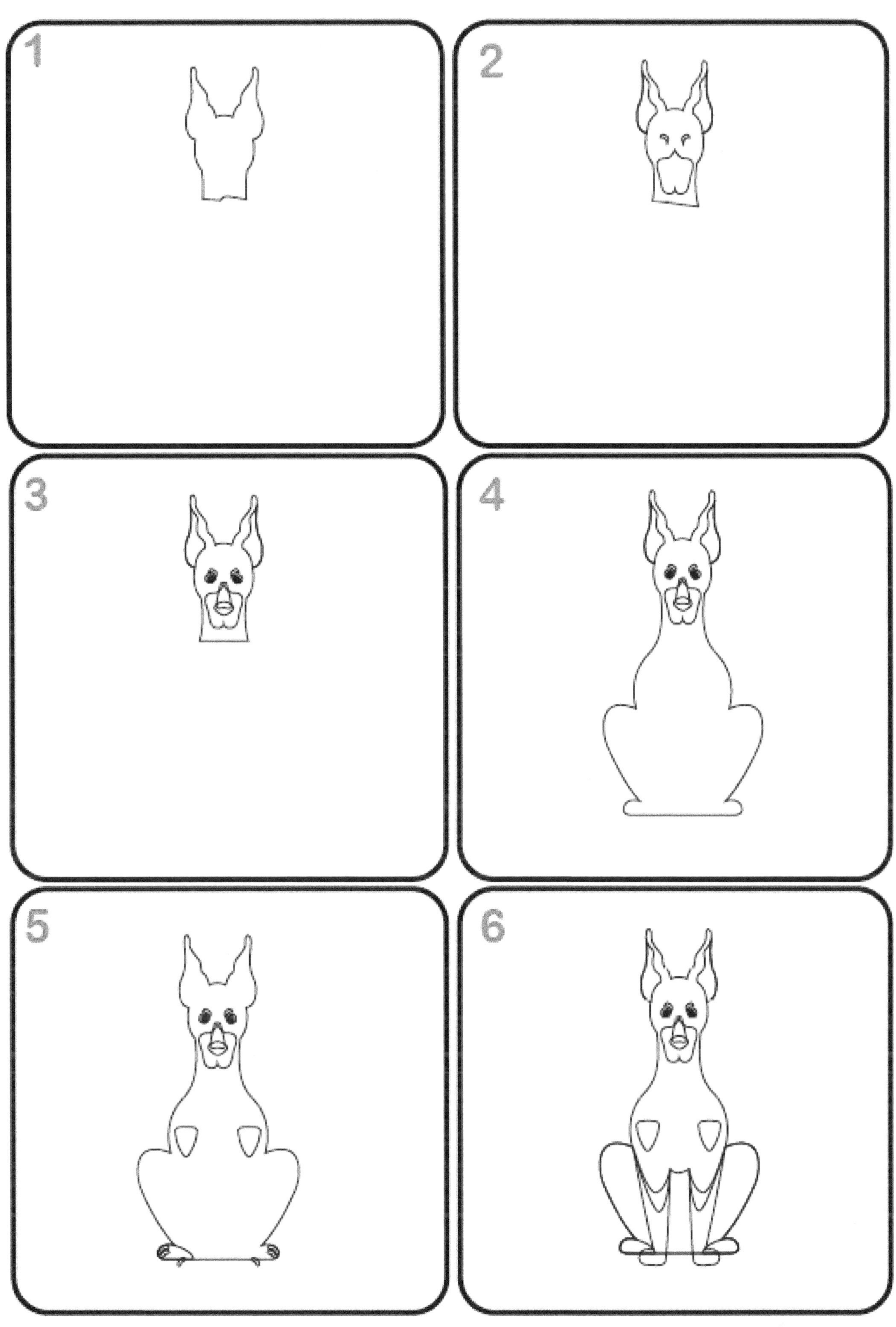

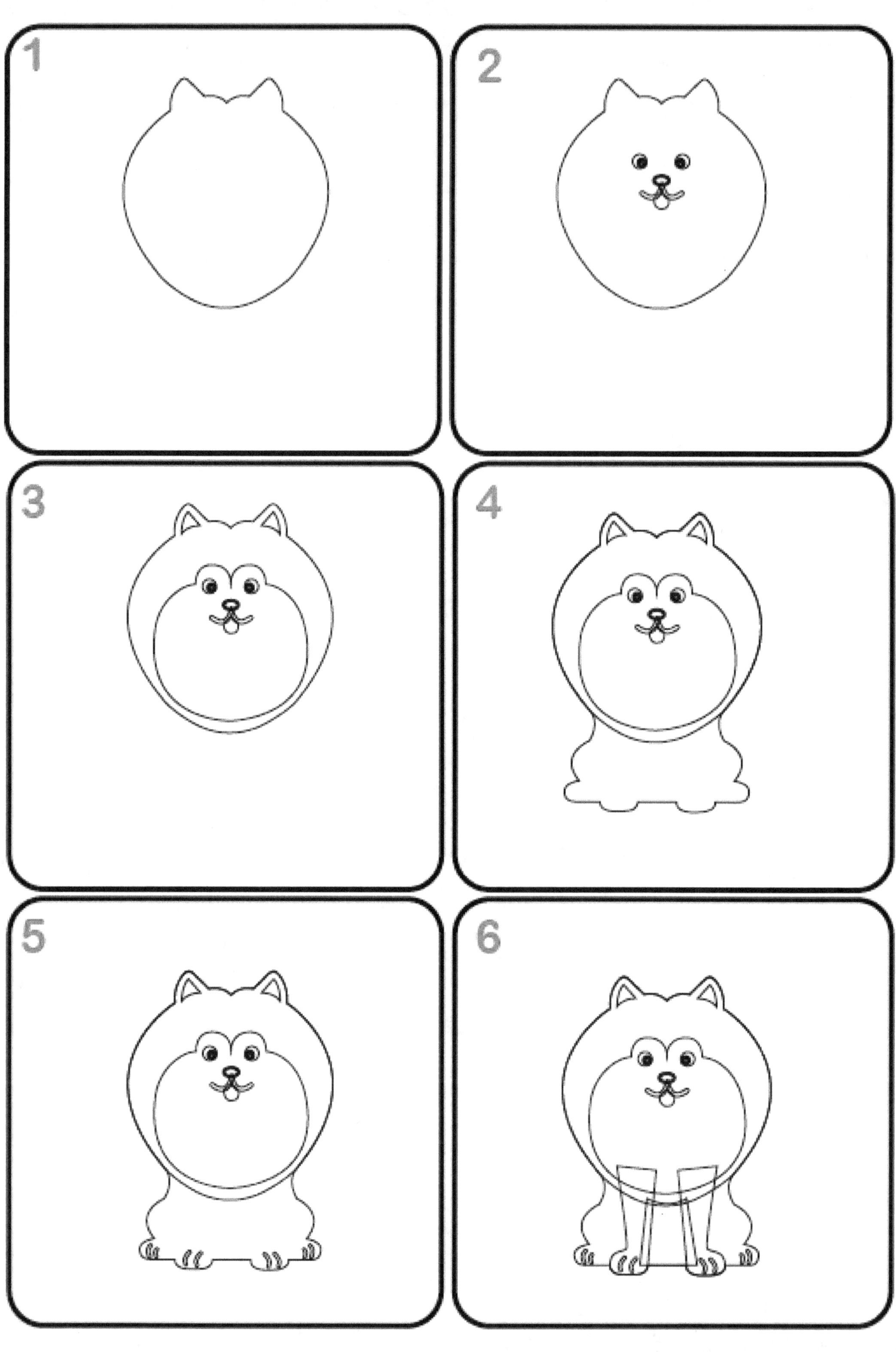

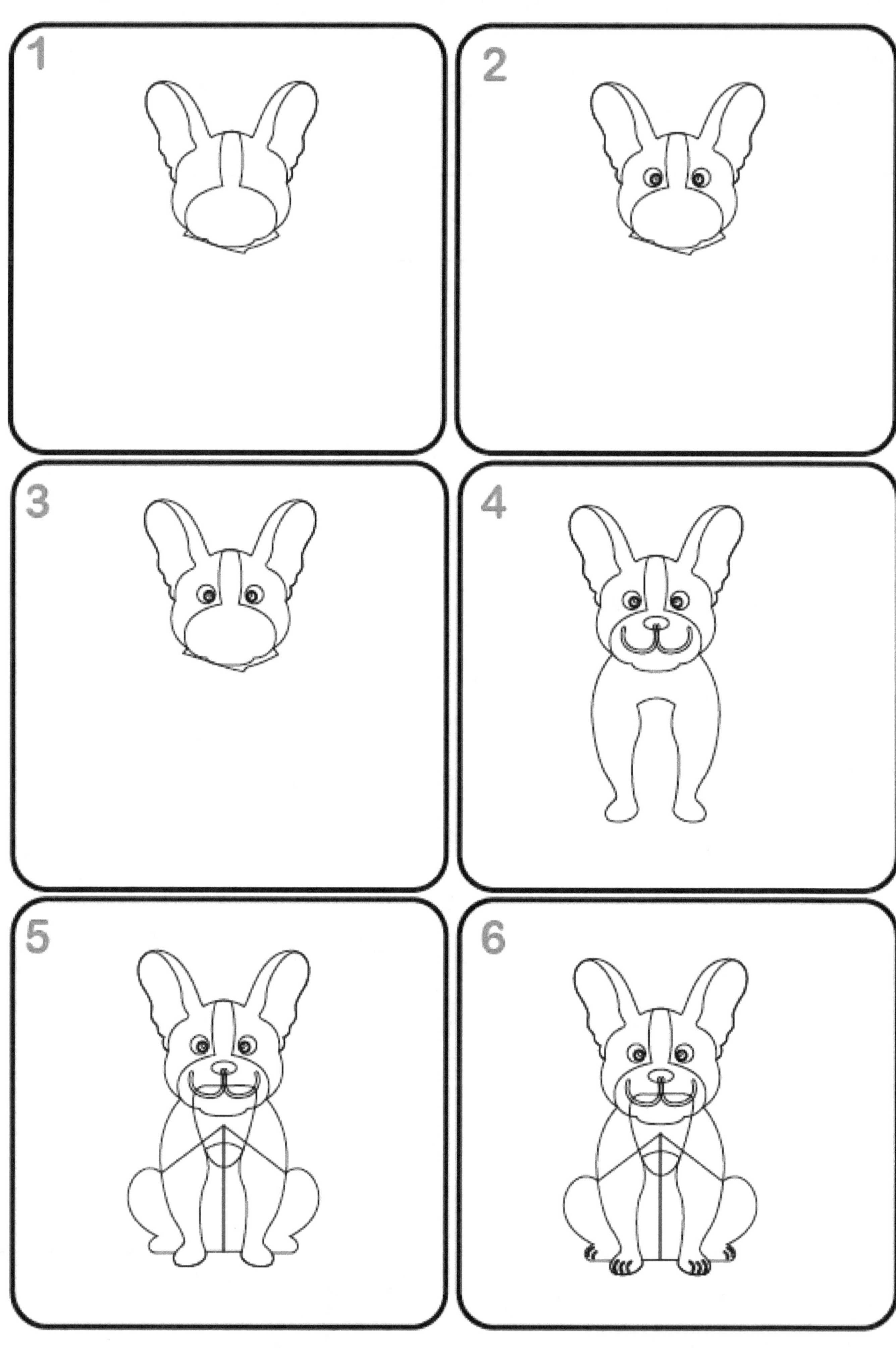

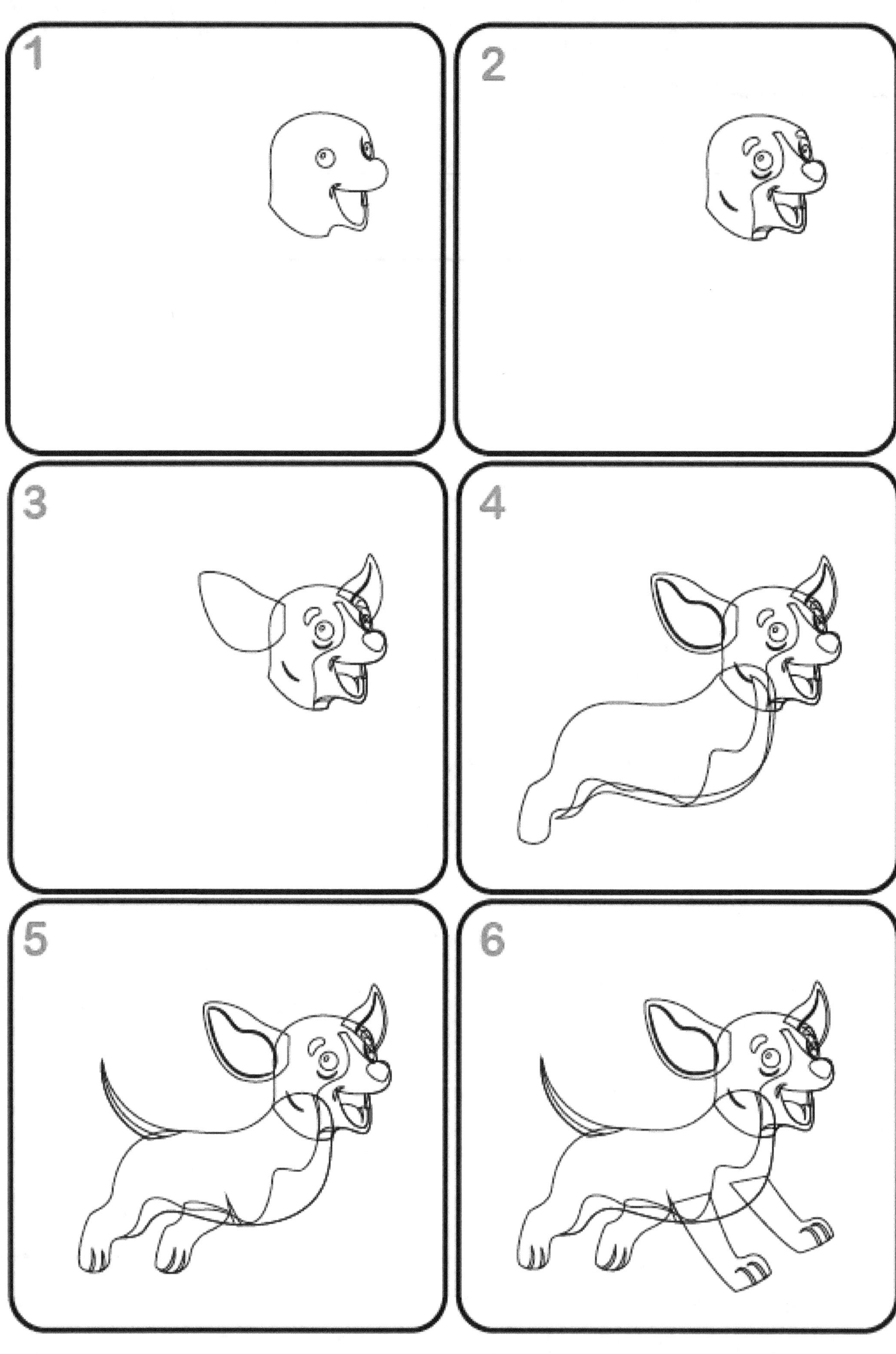

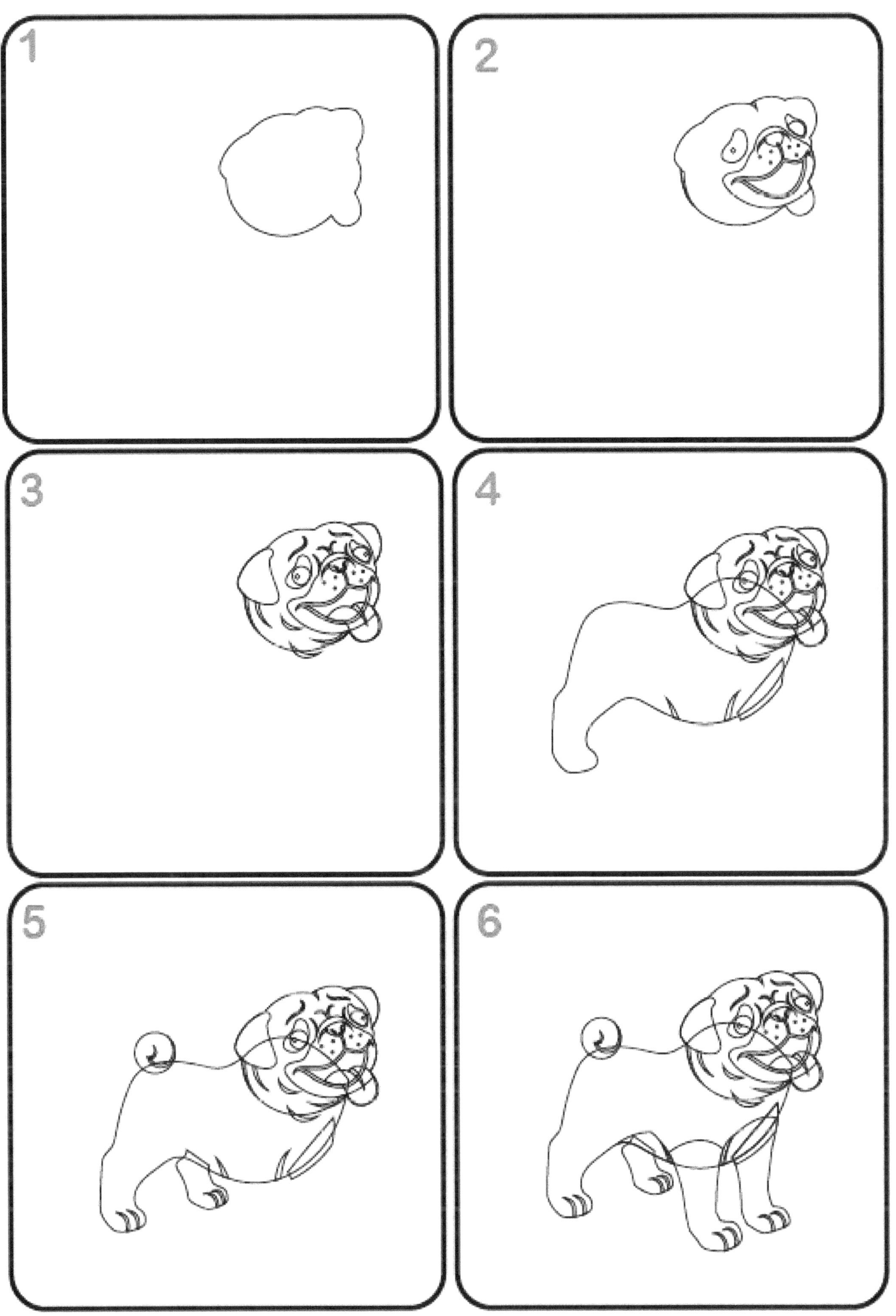

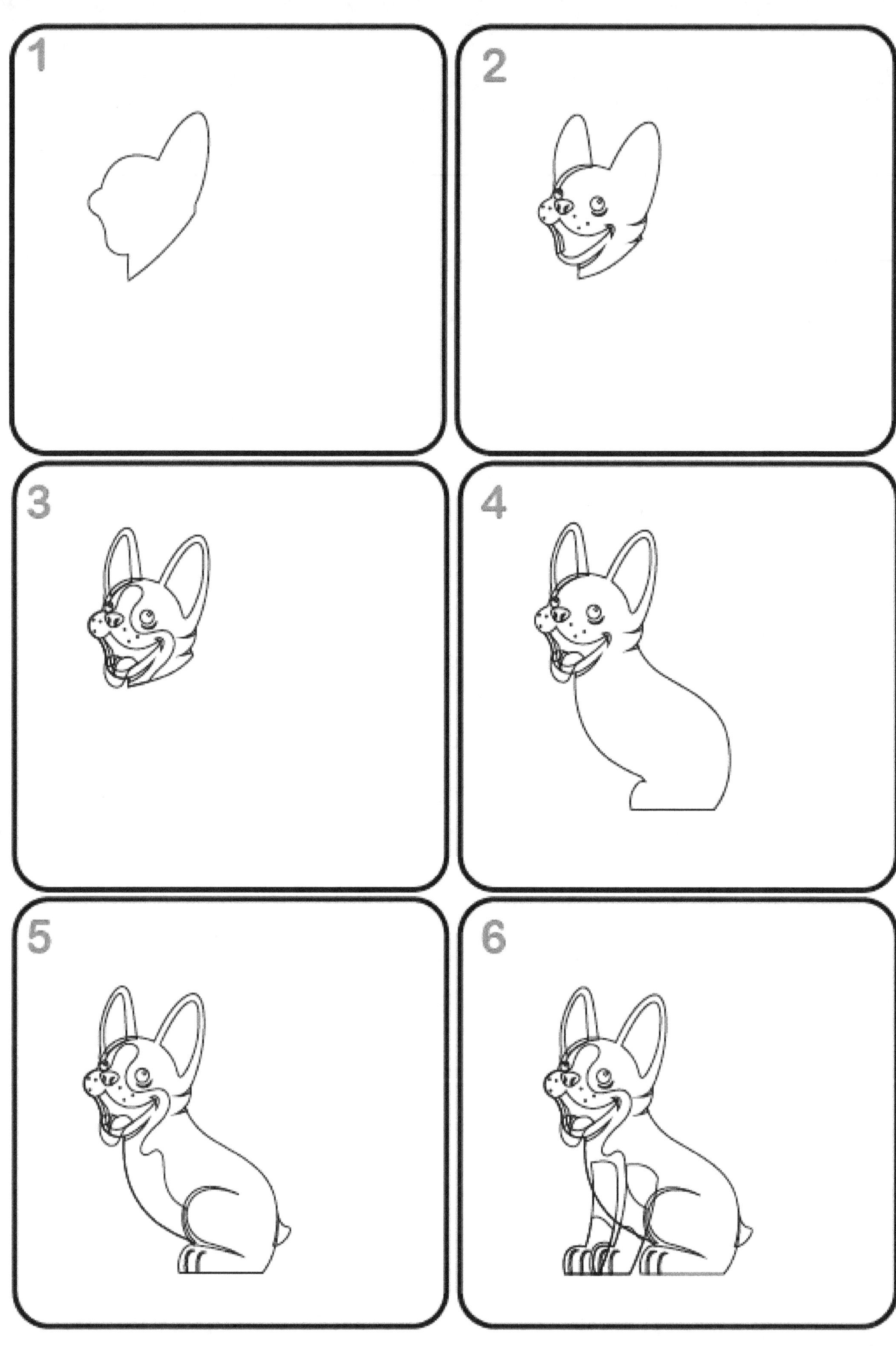

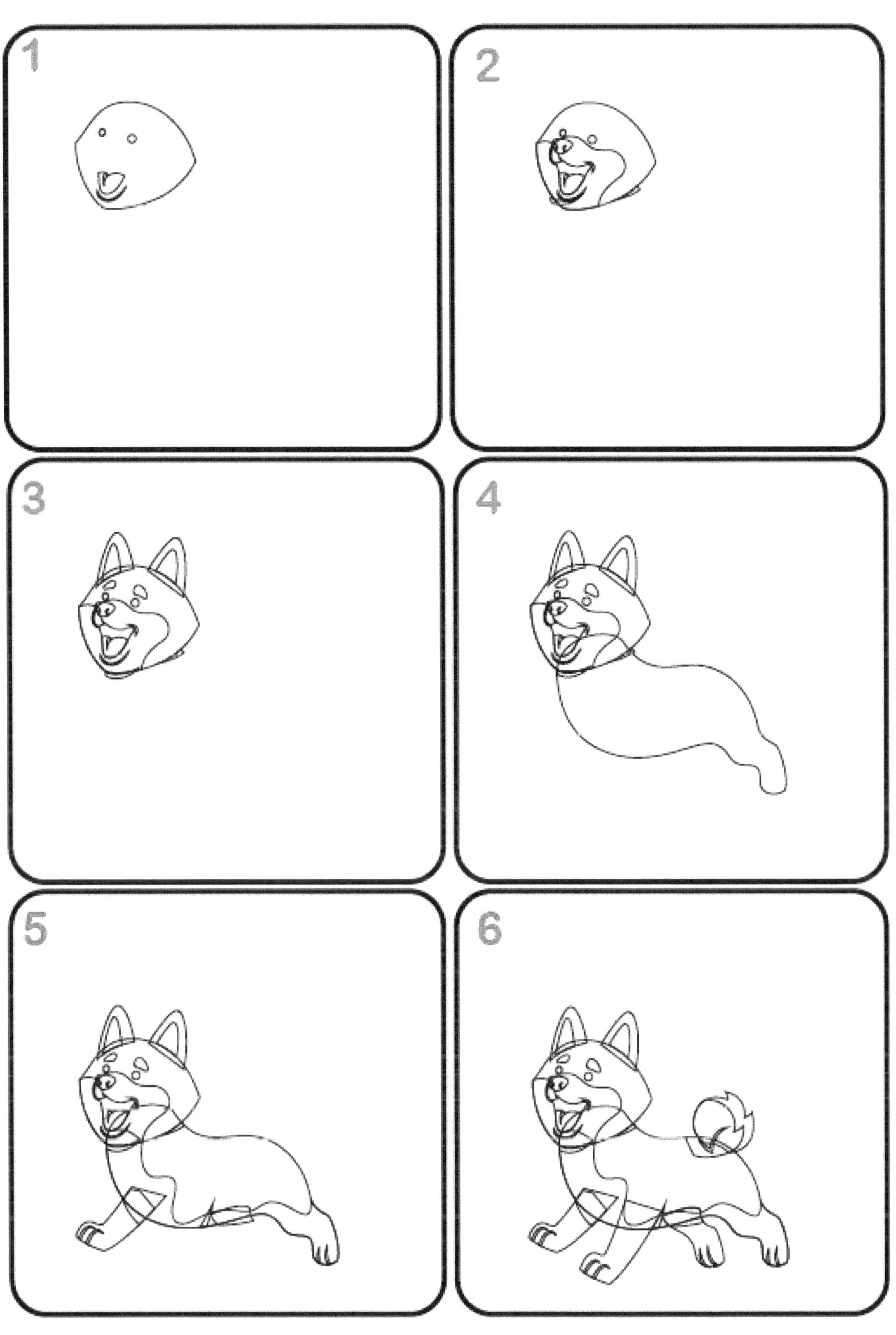

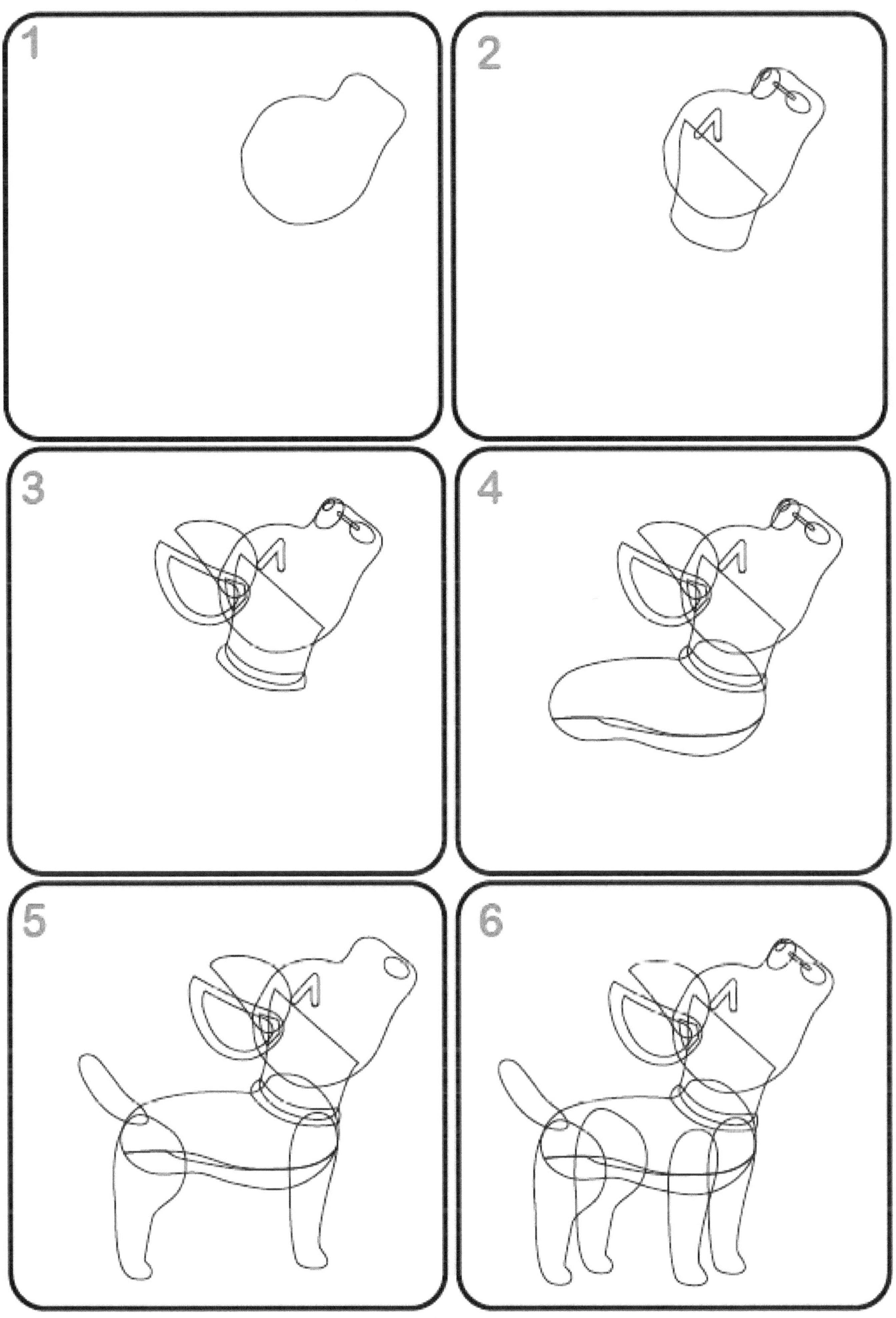

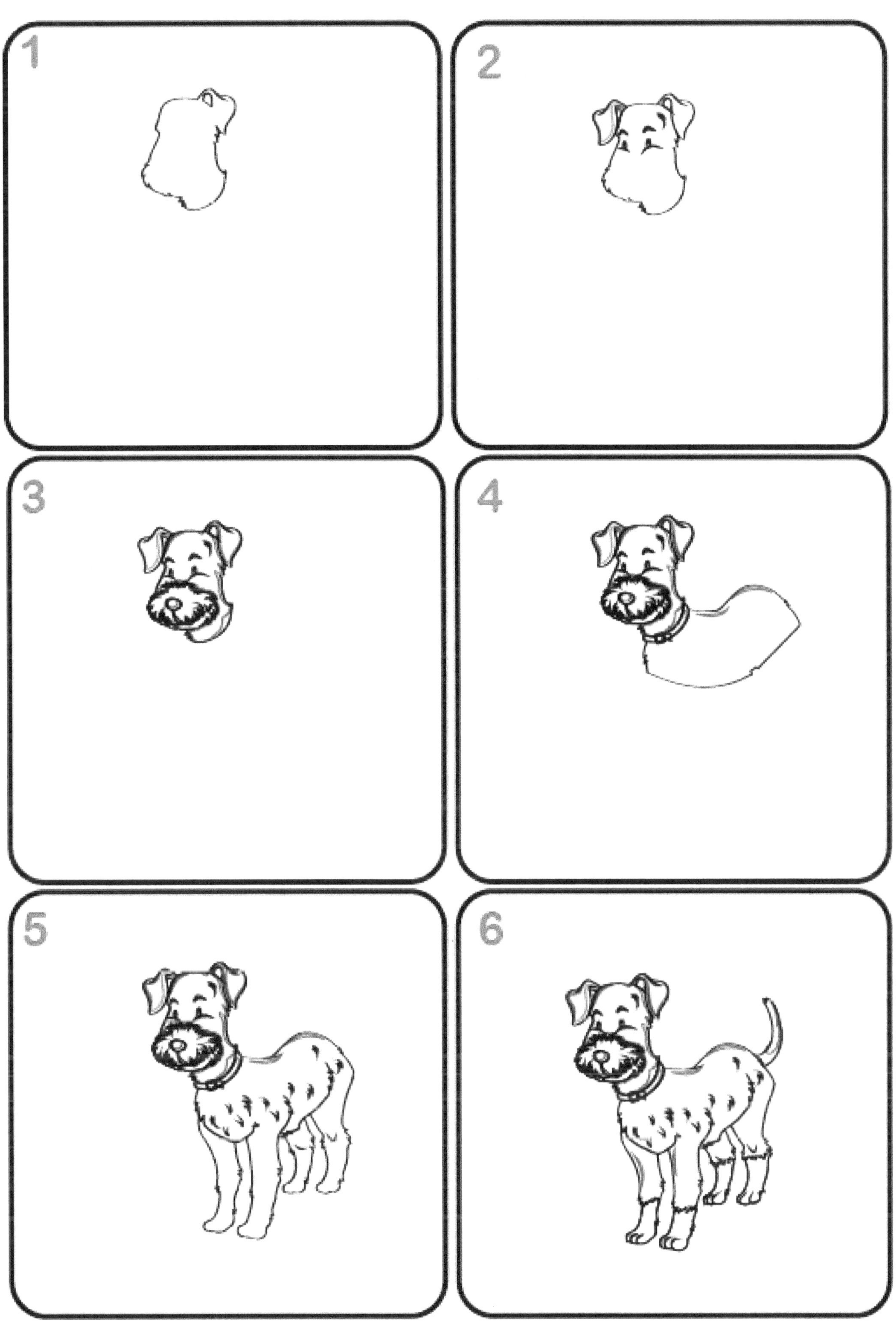

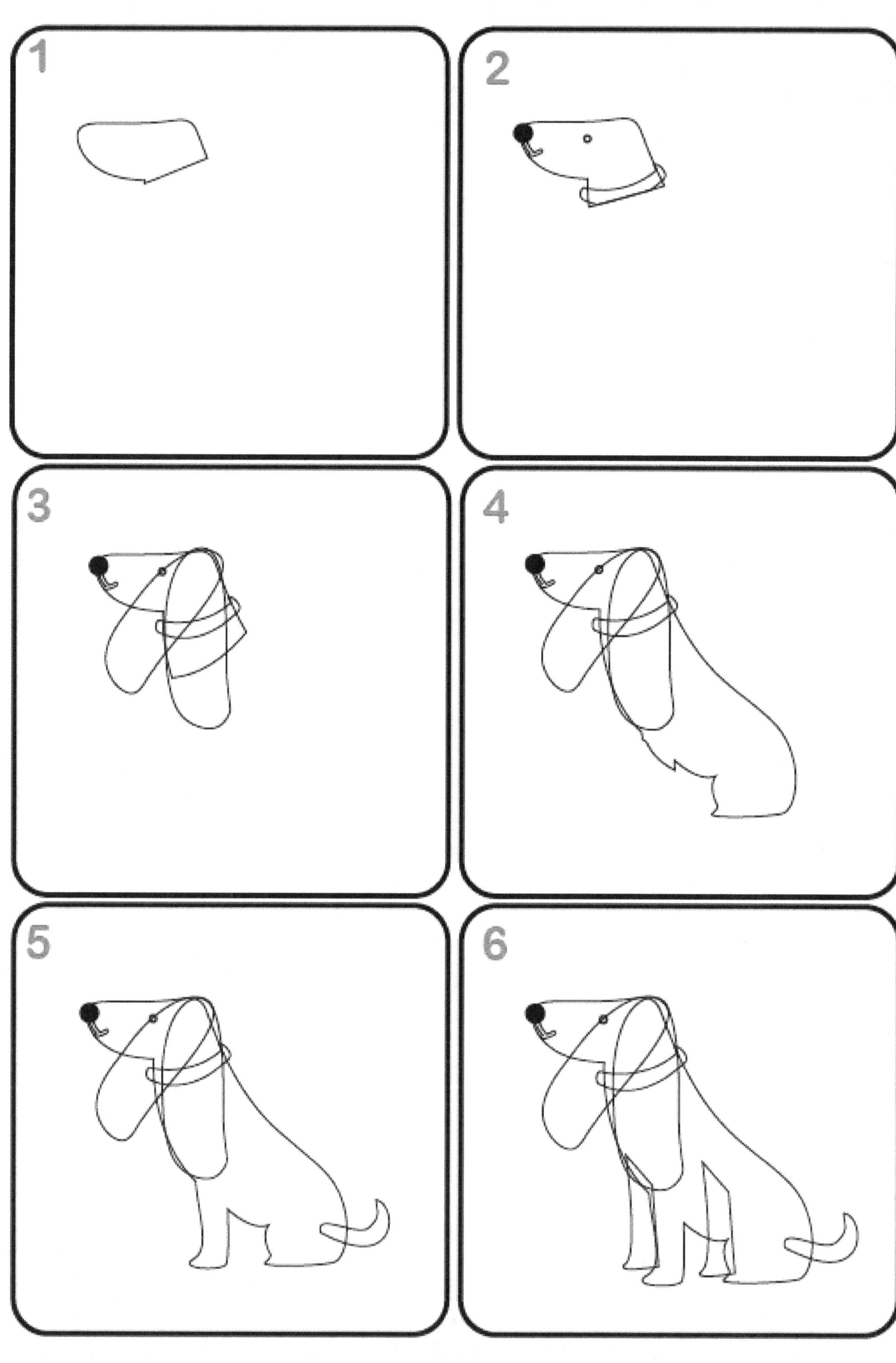